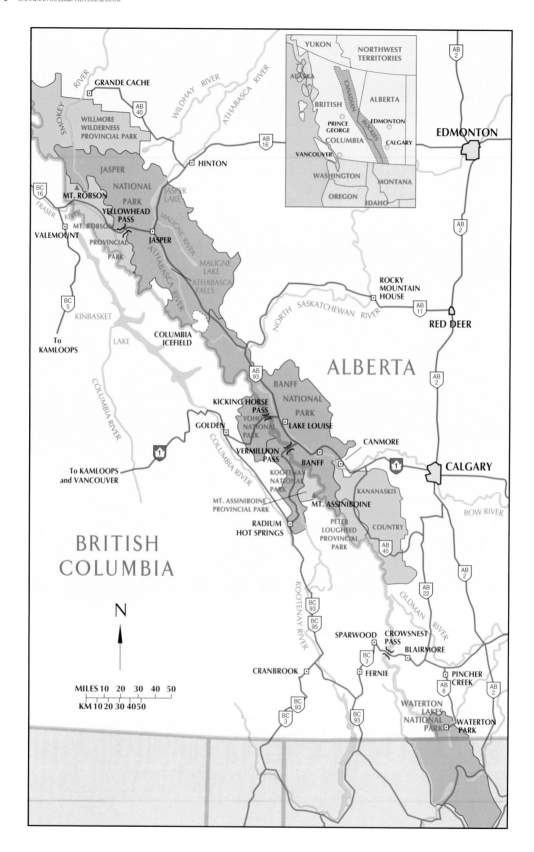

*Previous page: Banff Avenue under Cascade Mountain, Banff National Park*

# THE CANADIAN ROCKIES
## • PICTORIAL BOOK •

*Waterton Lakes National Park.*

In attempting to describe the vastness of the Canadian Rockies travelers have called it a "frozen ocean" or a "sea of peaks." Others have referred to it as a "vertical world" or a place where "the world stands on end." It is this ever-changing profile of peaks against the sky which dominates a visitor's first impressions and provides a constant source of visual interest. Not only do the mountains change shape drastically when viewed from different angles, they can also appear quite different when seen at different seasons or times of day. Some say, if fact, that it is hard to experience the same peak twice.

The National Parks of the Canadian Rockies are linked by major highways which allow easy access for the visitor and the opportunity to experience the majestic mountain environment at any time of the year.

Waterton Lakes National Park is the most southernly of the mountain National Parks. It touches the border with the United States and is part of the International Peace Park, including Waterton on the Canadian side and Glacier Park on the American side. In fact, the boat trip down Waterton Lake crosses the border from Canada into the United States—without going through customs!

The town of Waterton is open during the summer months and boasts a number of excellent restaurants and accomodations, including the Prince of Wales hotel which, as can be seen in the photograph above, is situated on a promintory of land overlooking the lake.

# • BANFF •

Banff, located 20 kilometers from Canmore, is nestled at the foot of Rundle, Cascade, Sulphur, and Tunnel Mountains. Mount Rundle was named after the Reverend Robert Rundle, a Methodist missionary to the Plains Indians who visited this area in 1847. Cascade Mountain was named by Sir James Hector who climbed the peak and camped at its base in 1858. Although the present Banff town site was well known to the early explorers of the Canadian Rockies it wasn't until the Canadian Pacific Railway came in the 1880's that the town of Banff was born. The discovery by railway workers of hot mineral springs on Sulphur Mountain in 1883 not only brought about the creation of a National Park, but also highlighted the C.P.R.'s promotion of the new transcontinental railway.

The Banff Springs Hotel was built on the slopes of Sulphur Mountain and first opened for business in 1888. Billed as "The Finest Hotel on the North American Continent," it attracted tourists from around the world. Carriage roads allowed travel in the area and businesses began developing on the north shore of the Bow River to provide additional services to the tourists.

The mountains around Banff were some of the earliest explored in the Rockies as the new railway brought vacationers and hikers to the area. The C.P.R. imported Swiss guides to help attract European climbers. As a result, a tremendous number of first ascents were registered by the turn of the century.

The Banff Springs Hotel overlooks the Bow Valley. Nearby are the Bow Falls, a popular sight for early explorers as well as present-day visitors. Tunnel Mountain is the home of the Hoodoos, strange erosion-sculpted pillars of rock.

Banff owes its existence to hot mineral springs. The Upper Hot Springs, located on Sulphur Mountain, are open year round. They are slightly warmer than the Cave and Basin Springs and have a distinctive smell due to the sulphur content of the water. The Sulphur Mountain Gondola Lift (also open year round) starts beside the Upper Hot Springs and the journey to the top provides an excellent view of the Banff town site and the Bow River Valley. There is a restaurant at the summit of Sulphur Mountain.

*Cascade Mountain and the Town of Banff from the top of Sulphur Mountain.*

*Mt. Rundle is reflected in the still waters of the first Vermilion Lake near the town of Banff.*

*A horse-drawn carriage mingles with the traffic on Banff Avenue. Cascade Mountain is in the background.*

*The Bow Valley with the Fairholme Range in the background is the view from the Banff Springs Hotel.*

*The Bow Falls lie just below the Banff Springs Hotel.*

**Opposite: The Banff Springs Hotel.**

*This view of Cascade Mountain is from the flower gardens at the Banff Park Administration Building.*

There are a host of activities available to the Banff summer visitor. The 18 hole golf course at the Banff Springs Hotel is world famous not only for its championship quality but also for its unique mountain setting. Bowling and indoor miniture golf can also be found at the Banff Springs. Boating and fishing is popular at nearby Lake Minnewanka, as is canoeing on the Bow River and hiking on the numerous trails that radiate from Banff.

The Whyte Foundation is located in downtown Banff. It contains a museum of the Canadian Rockies, an archives and the Banff Historic Homes which collectively provide

*Elk are one of the most common sights in the town of Banff.*

insights into the history and development of the region. The Luxton Museum in Banff offers extensive Native and wildlife displays. The Natural History Museum in Central Park near the Bow River bridge interprets the flora, fauna and geology of the area. The Banff Center, situated above the town site on Tunnel Mountain, offers year-round advanced programs in music, theatre, and the visual arts.

The town of Banff is also an excellent place to view elk. These large animals are an everyday sight for the residents of Banff. They can be dangerous, however, especially during rutting and calving season. Every-one is warned to keep their distance.

*The Cave and Basin.*

*The Upper Hot Springs on Sulphur Mountain.*

*The Hoodoos as seen from Tunnel Mountain Drive.*

*Lake Minnewanka near the town of Banff.*

*A field of yellow flowers stretches beneath Castle Mountain in Banff National Park.*

Motorists traveling west of Banff can enjoy the excellent views along the Trans-Canada Highway. Castle Mountain is one of the best-known mountains in this area. Aptly named by early mountain explorer Sir James Hector, this turreted, castellate-type peak reminds many visitors of a medieval fortress.

An alternative route west which goes as far as Lake Louise is the 1-A Highway. This road allows a more intimate experience of the valley and forest environment. Johnston Canyon is located on the 1-A Highway a few kilometers east of Castle Mountain. Excellent nature trails lead to the Lower Falls as well as to the Upper Falls and the Ink Pots. The trail to the lower falls allows wheelchair access. At places it is dramatically cantilevered over the river below.

Mt. Temple is the highest mountain in Banff National Park. Since it is not a difficult mountain to climb, technically speaking, many early surveyors used this peak to help them get an overview of the entire area.

**Opposite: A footbridge at the Lower Falls of Johnston Canyon crosses the river to a small cave which affords a dramatic, close-up view of the falls.**

*Mt. Temple is located near Lake Louise.*

# • MORAINE LAKE •

Moraine Lake in the Valley of the Ten Peaks is almost as famous as Lake Louise. Located a few kilometers east of Lake Louise, Moraine Lake reflects the Wenkchemna Peaks. These mountains take their name from the Stoney word for "ten". Moraine Lake itself gets its name from the heap of rock debris which acts as a dam at the bottom of the lake. Walter Wilcox, who discovered this lake in the 1890's, mistakenly thought that this rock pile was a moraine from an earlier glacier. It is now believed to be the product of a large rock slide from the Tower of Babel which looms directly above it.

A lodge, situated on the shore of Moraine Lake, offers accommodation and meals during the summer season. There are, as well, many hiking trails throughout this area. The trail to Consolation Lake is a short 3 km walk which skirts the eastern flank of the Tower of Babel. The trails to Larch Valley and to Eiffel Lake, while somewhat longer, provide excellent panoramas of the Valley of the Ten Peaks.

*Moraine Lake lies just to the east of Lake Louise.*

*Moraine Lake in the Valley of the Ten Peaks*

# • LAKE LOUISE •

Tom Wilson, a packer for the Canadian Pacific Railway, first laid eyes on Lake Louise in 1882. Ever since there has been a constant influx of explorers, climbers and tourists, claiming it the most beautiful place they have seen. The C.P.R. built a chalet on the shores of the lake in 1890 and used the lake as part of its promotion for the new railway. In time the chalet was developed into a major hotel known as the Chateau Lake Louise. In 1894 the Yale Lake Louise Club began extensive explorations in the area. They produced the first detailed map of the Lake Louise region as well as the first major book on the Canadian Rockies. From 1912 to 1930 a tramway transported guests from the railway station to the Chateau.

Lake Louise was created by a glacier. At one time the Victoria Glacier stretched to the site of the present Chateau. Here it deposited debris which accumulated to form what is called a terminal moraine. This moraine acted as a dam so that when the glacier retreated, the meltwaters were trapped and formed Lake Louise. The emerald green colour of the lake is due to the fine particles of glacial silt suspended in the water which reflect the green rays of the spectrum. A hiking trail leads along the north shore of the lake, through the gap and up to a magnificent over-view of Mount Victoria and what remains of the Victoria Glacier. A teahouse is located near the end of the trail and is open during the summer season for refreshments.

In 1924 the original wooden Chateau was destroyed by fire. It was replaced the following year by the present day structure, which remained unchanged for almost 60 years until the exterior of the hotel was resurfaced in 1984-1985. The hotel has always taken pride in its flower gardens on the grounds. Icelandic and Shirley poppies are a particular tradition, introduced to the Chateau early in the century.

*The grounds of the Chateau Lake Louise are adorned with magnificent flower gardens.*

*One of the charms of Lake Louise is the Chateau that graces its lakeside.*

*Lake Louise is a year-round destination. In winter, skiers flock to the world-class Lake Louise ski area.*

**Next page: Lake Louise from the lakeside trail.**

# • YOHO •

om Wilson, the first white man to see Lake Louise, was also the first to set eyes on what is now called Emerald Lake. Wilson's discovery was passed on to the C. P. Railroad and a lodge was built to accommodate travelers. Emerald Lake's magnificent colour is due to the presence of glacial silt suspended in the water. A trail leads around the lake affording the visitor splendid views of the lake in its mountain setting.

Along the Emerald Lake Road lies the Natural Bridge where the Kicking Horse River has eroded a hole in the limestone rock allowing the entire river to pass through a narrow slit.

Perhaps the most stunning sight in Yoho is Takakkaw Falls—the highest waterfall in Canada, where meltwater from the Daly Glacier falls hundreds of feet over a sheer limestone cliff on its way to join the Yoho River. The name *Takakkaw* comes from the Stoney word meaning "It is wonderful." Access to the falls is by a road which junctions with the Trans Canada Highway a few miles east of Field, B.C.

*The Natural Bridge over the Kicking Horse River.*

*Emerald Lake is the sight of a beautiful resort which includes an historic main lodge built from logs.*

**Opposite: Takakkaw Falls in Yoho Valley.**

# • ICEFIELD PARKWAY •

One of the dreams of A. O. Wheeler, founder of the Alpine Club of Canada, was a road connecting Banff and Jasper. After traveling the route with a pack-train in 1911, he prophecized that "this wonder trail will be world renowned". His prophecy came true in 1940 when the Icefield Parkway was completed, allowing thousands of travelers access to the grandeur and beauty that has made it famous.

Traveling from the south, you pass Crowfoot Glacier which takes its name from its distinctive "toes" which resemble the foot of a crow. Although the bottom-most toe broke off in the 1940's due to the consistent retreat of this glacier, the resemblance is still close enough to do justice to the name.

Just north of Crowfoot Glacier lies Bow Lake, which finds its source in the Bow Glacier which can be seen at the head of the valley which leads into the north end of the lake. Num-ti-jah Lodge, located on the shore of Bow Lake, was built by Jimmy Simpson, a pioneer outfitter and guide. The lodge, which was constructed a number of years before the advent of the Parkway, offers accommodation and meals.

A few kilometers north of Bow Lake lies the Mistaya Valley and a spectacular view of Peyto Lake. It was named after the legendary guide, Bill Peyto, renowned for his skills at guiding pack-trains traveling north from Lake Louise along the route of the present highway. Howse Peak and Mount Chephren lie a few kilometers north of Peyto Lake.

*The red roof of Num-ti-jah lodge can be seen in this aerial view of Bow Lake.*

*The snow-capped mountains of the Lake Louise area can be seen reflected in the waters of Herbert Lake.*

*Crowfoot Glacier is a popular sight along the Icefield Parkway.*

*From the viewpoint on Bow Summit, provides this view of Peyto Lake and the Mistaya Valley.*

*Mt. Chephren rises majestically above the still waters of Waterfowl Lake on the Icefield Parkway.*

*Athabasca Glacier is one of the highlights of the Icefield Parkway.*

The most famous landmark along the Icefield Parkway is the Athabasca Glacier. It is located in Jasper National Park just north of the Park boundary. Athabasca Glacier is just one of many massive glaciers which flow down from the immense Columbia icefield. The Icefield, not visible from the highway, lies beyond the headwall of Athabasca Glacier. Meltwater from the Icefield eventually flows into three separate oceans.

Athabasca Glacier is one of the few places in the world where motorists can park just yards away from an active glacier. It is possible to climb upon the ice and experience a glacier firsthand. Snowmobile tours are available for those wishing a more

*Snowmobile tours on Athabasca Glacier.*

relaxed adventure. The large "ridges" of rock on either side of the glacier are called moraines and consist of bits of rock carried along by the glacier. As the glacier retreats, these moraines are left behind and indicate the extent of the ice years ago. At the turn of the century, Athabasca Glacier extended across the valley to the site of the present Columbia Icefield Chalet. The Chalet is open during the summer season and provides meals and accommodation. The Columbia Icefield Information Bureau, just to the north of the Chalet is run by Jasper National Park interpretive service. Displays, photographs and films provide visitors with a better understanding of the unique world of glaciers.

**Next page: The Columbia Icefield Chalet and the Athabasca Glacier.**

*Sunwapta Falls on the Athabasca River.*

*Athabasca Falls with Mt. Kerkeslin behind.*

Traveling north along the Icefield parkway, the road follows the Sunwapta River whose headwaters start at the Athabasca Glacier. The word Sunwapta means "turbulent river" in the native Stoney language.

At Sunwapta Falls the river plunges into a deep canyon before it joins the Athabasca River. This area was extensively explored by Professor A. P. Coleman in 1892 and 1893 in his search for two legendary peaks once thought to tower over Athabasca Pass. A few miles north of Sunwapta Falls and west of the Parkway is Mount Fryatt which, at 3,360 meters, is one of the highest peaks in the area.

To the east rises Mount Kerkeslin with its prominent lateral ridges of sedimentary rock. At the foot of Mount Kerkeslin are the Athabasca Falls, another of the dramatic sights on the Parkway. The bridge over the river below the falls provides an excellent view of the thundering water. The name "Athabasca" comes from the Cree language and means "where there are reeds". This is a reference to the marshy delta of the river at the point where it runs into Lake Athabasca.

Mt. Edith Cavell is the most imposing peak in the area around Jasper. So prominent is its summit that the mountain used to be called "La Montagne de la Grand Traverse" (the mountain of the great crossing) and was used as a landmark and navigational point by the voyageurs and fur traders as they paddled up the Athabasca River on their way towards Athabasca Pass and the interior of British Columbia. Mount Edith Cavell was renamed after World War I to honour a heroic British nurse.

Angel Glacier hangs on the cliffs of Mt.Edith Cavell, suspended above the valley floor as if by magic. Angel Glacier is a classic example of a hanging glacier.

*Mt. Kerkeslin looms above Horseshoe Lake.*

*Mt. Edith Cavell is reflected in the waters of Cavell lake.*

# • JASPER •

Lying in the broad valley of the Athabasca River at the junction of the Icefield Parkway and the Yellowhead Highway, the town of Jasper is the northern focal point of the Rocky Mountains. This area has an older recorded history than the Southern Rockies, beginning in the early nineteenth century with fur traders traveling on the Athabasca River and Athabasca Pass on their way to central British Columbia. Later the lower and less arduous Yellowhead Pass was used which is now the route of the Yellowhead Highway and the Canadian National Railway.

In 1811 the first fur trading post in the mountains was built near the present Jasper town site and christened Henry's House after William Henry, a Northwest Company trader. Jasper House (after Jasper Hawes, a local trapper) was later built on the Athabasca River. When the fur trade waned, the old routes were forgotten and trading posts fell into disrepair. Not until mid-century did civilization touch the area once more. In the 1850's Henry Moberly rebuilt Jasper House and a settlement sprang up around it. In 1872 Sir Sandford Fleming, Engineer-in-chief of the C.P.R. Surveys, proposed Yellowhead Pass for the new transcontinental railway route through the Rockies.

Politics prevailed over common sense and the difficult southern route over the Rogers Pass was chosen. In expectation of a second railway line over Yellowhead Pass, Jasper Park was established in 1907. When the Grand Trunk line reached the park in 1911 the town of Fitzhugh sprang up and two years later changed its name to Jasper. Civilization had finally come to stay.

The Jasper Skytram is located on Whistler Mountain and may be reached by road starting from the Icefield Parkway, 2.4 kilometers south of the Jasper town site. After an exciting ride to the top of the Tramway, a spectacular panorama unfolds stretching from the town of Jasper to the distant Mount Robson, 80 kilometers to the west. Refreshments are available in the upper terminal and a walking trail may be followed to the actual summit.

The town of Jasper grew rapidly after the coming of the railway. To accommodate the new inhabitants, a tent city was erected on the shore of Lac Beauvert. Today this same site boasts the luxurious Jasper Park Lodge, a Canadian National Railroad hotel built in the 1920's. The Jasper Park Lodge offers a wide range of activities for its guests including an 18 hole golf course, swimming, and boating.

*The town of Jasper lies nestled in the valley beneath the Jasper Tramway.*

*The Jasper Park Lodge can be seen across the waters of Lac Beauvert.*

*The Park Information building in downtown Jasper is a unique stone and log structure.*

*Pyramid Mountain shimmers in the water of Pyramid Lake near the town of Jasper.*

*One of Maligne Canyon's many dramatic sights.*

The mountains surrounding the peaceful Athabasca Valley contain some of the most spectacular spots in the Canadian Rockies. A beautiful drive is the road through the Maligne valley to Maligne Lake.

At Maligne Canyon, one of the most unique spots in the valley, a nature trail allows visitors a close-up view of the tremendous weathered gorges made by the Maligne River. The road continues along the shores of Medicine Lake. This lake, set in a depression which resembles a medicine basin (hence its name) tends to fluctuate in level throughout the year. As there is no visible outlet for the water, the lake must drain through the bedrock, further emphasizing its resemblance to a sink. The road ends at Maligne Lake itself where a lodge offers refreshments and accommodation. Boat trips are available for tours to the far end of the Lake. Here can be found the world-famous view of Spirit Island, one of the Rockies' most famous views.

The name *Maligne* is derived from the French word "maline", meaning "bad". The name was given by an early explorer who obviously found the travel near the lake to be especially difficult. Mary Schaeffer travelled the length of the lake on a raft fashioned with logs from the surrounding forests. During her famous trip, she named most of the mountains for her close friends and companions.

*Spirit Island is near the south end of Maligne Lake and is only accessible by boat.*

*The spectacular peaks surrounding Spirit Island were named by the early explorer, Mary Schaeffer.*

*Mt. Robson is the highest peak in the Canadian Rockies.*

Mt. Robson is located in Robson Provincial Park, not quite 100 kilometres west of the town of Jasper along the Yellowhead highway. At 3,954 metres, Mt. Robson is easily the highest peak in the Canadian Rockies.

It was first climbed in 1909 by Reverend Kinney and "Curly" Phillips. These two were only a few metres short of the summit when they were forced back by bad weather. The first successful climb was by Konrad Kain in 1913.

Today Robson is a popular climb for adventurous mountaineers. The mountain, however, is still famous for attracting clouds and stormy weather which can develop very quickly and can cause climbers a considerable degree of discomfort.

*A Rocky Mountain Bighorn sheep.*